POETRY

September 2014

FOUNDED IN 1912 BY HARRIET MONROE

VOLUME CCIV ' NUMBER 5

CONTENTS

September 2014

POEMS

FREEDOM OF SHADOW

COMMENT

Editor	DON SHARE
Art Director	FRED SASAKI
Managing Editor	SARAH DODSON
Assistant Editor	LINDSAY GARBUTT
Editorial Assistant	HOLLY AMOS
Consulting Editor	CHRISTINA PUGH
Design	ALEXANDER KNOWLTON

COVER ART BY SONNENZIMMER
"Cromwell Dixon's Elements of Flight," 2010

POETRYMAGAZINE.ORG

A PUBLICATION OF THE
POETRY FOUNDATION
PRINTED BY CADMUS PROFESSIONAL COMMUNICATIONS, US

Poetry · *September 2014* · *Volume 204* · *Number 5*

Poetry (ISSN: 0032-2032) is published monthly, except bimonthly July/August, by the Poetry Foundation. Address editorial correspondence to 61 W. Superior St., Chicago, IL 60654. Individual subscription rates: $35.00 per year domestic; $47.00 per year foreign. Library/institutional subscription rates: $38.00 per year domestic; $50.00 per year foreign. Single copies $3.75, plus $1.75 postage, for current issue; $4.25, plus $1.75 postage, for back issues. Address new subscriptions, renewals, and related correspondence to Poetry, PO 421141, Palm Coast, FL 32142-1141 or call 800.327.6976. Periodicals postage paid at Chicago, IL, and additional mailing offices. POSTMASTER: Send address changes to Poetry, PO Box 421141, Palm Coast, FL 32142-1141. All rights reserved. Copyright © 2014 by the Poetry Foundation. Double issues cover two months but bear only one number. Volumes that include double issues comprise numbers 1 through 5. Please visit poetryfoundation.org/poetrymagazine/submissions for submission guidelines and to access the magazine's online submission system. Available in braille from the National Library Service for the Blind and Physically Handicapped. Available on microfilm and microfiche through National Archive Publishing Company, Ann Arbor, MI. Digital archive available at JSTOR. org. Distributed to bookstores by Ingram Periodicals, Ubiquity Distributors, and Central Books in the UK.

POEMS

JOHN ASHBERY

Bunch of Stuff

To all events I squirted you
knowing this not to be this came to pass
when we were out and it looked good.
Why wouldn't you want a fresh piece
of outlook to stand in down the years?
See, your house, a former human energy construction,
crashed with us for a few days in May
and sure enough, the polar inscape
brought about some easier poems,
which I guessed was a good thing. At least
some of us were relaxed, Steamboat Bill included.

He didn't drink nothing.
It was one thing
to be ready for their challenge, quite another to accept it.
And if I had a piece of advice for you, this is it:
Poke fun at balm, then suffer lethargy
to irradiate its shallow flood in the new packaging
our enemies processed. They should know.

The Gold Dust Twins never stopped supplicating Hoosiers
to limn the trail. There's no Shakespeare.
Through the window, Casanova.
Couldn't get to sleep in the dumb incident
of those days, crimping the frozen feet of Lincoln.

Alms for the Beekeeper

He makes better errors that way.
Pass it around at breakfast:
the family and all, down there with a proximate sense of power,
lawyering up. Less log-heavy, your text-strategy
beat out other options, is languid.
Duets in the dust start up,
begin. Again.

He entered the firm at night.
The 26th is a Monday.

By Guess and by Gosh

O awaken with me
the inquiring goodbyes.
Ooh what a messy business
a tangle and a muddle
(and made it seem quite interesting).

He ticks them off:
leisure top,
a different ride home,
whispering, in a way,
whispered whiskers,
so many of the things you have to share.

But I was getting on,
and that's what you don't need.
I'm certainly sorry about scaring your king,
if indeed that's what happened to him.
You get Peanuts and War and Peace,
some in rags, some in jags, some in
velvet gown. They want
the other side of the printing plant.

There were concerns.
Say hi to jock itch, leadership principles,
urinary incompetence.
Take that, perfect pitch.
And say a word for the president,
for the scholar magazines, papers, a streaming.
Then you are interested in poetry.

Dramedy

Things I left on your paper:
one of the craziest episodes that ever overtook me.
Do you like espionage? A watered charm?
My pod cast aside, I'll walk in the human street,
protect the old jib from new miniseries.

I could swear it moved
in incomplete back yards
to endorse the conversation, request to be strapped in.
Then it will be time to take the step
giving fragile responses,
and finally he wrote the day.

It happened in the water
so that was nice.

It comes ready conflated:
vanilla for get lost, flavor of the time
of his sponsor's destiny. Be on that sofa.

I was crossing the state line as they were reburying the stuff.
You break the time lock, the bride's canister...
but we did say that we'd be back.

Blueprints and Others

The man across the street seems happy,
or pleased. Sometimes a porter evades the grounds.
After you play a lot with the military
you are my own best customer.

I've done five of that.
Make my halloween. Ask me not to say it.
The old man wants to see you — *now*.
That's all right, but find your own.
Do you want to stop using these?

Last winning people told me to sit on the urinal.
Do not put on others what you can put on yourself.
How to be in the city my loved one.
Men in underwear … A biography field
like where we live in the mountains,

a falling. Yes I know you have.
Troves of merchandise, you know, "boomer buzz."
Hillbilly sculptures of the outside.
(They won't see anybody.)

Dandelions (II)

He drew
these dandelions
during one
of the days
when the only

solace
was derived
from the labor
of getting
the white stems

and blurry seed heads
just right. "Nobody there,"
the new disease
announced,
with black-tie gloom,

"nobody there,"
after he'd succumbed.
Sometimes,
sleeping soundly
is almost

unbearable.
Please take
care of me,
he asked,
as they put

his crayons
with his wallet
in a box
by the stove.
In the distance,

beyond the tulips,
an insect chorus
droned:
we beat you up;
we beat you up.

CATHERINE FIELD

Mythic Beaver

Yes, I'll haul your ashes
back to Oklahoma,
the Lord G-d of Abraham
riding shotgun.
I got the coffee sweats already,
just Him and me on 1-55,
you in a box on the seat between.

We aim for that dent in the dust
where your pa was born
in a sod stable
and your ma minced a snake
with a garden hoe;
that place the trappers named
Beaver, not thinking, for once,
of women.

Reminded too much of Texas,
G-d and I both hate
the cottonwoods
stuck to a high sky.
We share a drink,
swap our lies,
and sift out what we can
from the radio.

Your name comes up
and G-d's eyes get dusty.
When Gene Pitney sings
the "Sh'ma Yisrael,"
G-d stares out,
that box of ashes inside His jacket,
as close as He can hold it.

There's Beaver at nightfall,
and bean burritos
to wash down the beer.
We scatter your ashes
where we stop to pee,
the Lord G-d's laugh
steady as a train blows,
soft as lightning across the panhandle.

SYLVIA LEGRIS

Studies of an Ox's Heart, c. 1511–13

After Leonardo da Vinci

I

The long incision. The incipient voyage from aortic arch
to thoracic inlet. Small-particled is the corpuscled city.
(*Bustling opuscula.*) A city of animal electricity. A lowing
cycling mass. Calm the cowed heart. Still the browbeating
heart. Cool the controversial hearthstone. Let the blade
intervene where the divine intersects bovinity.

2

Pour wax into the gate of an ox's heart. Close the small
doors of the heart via a template of hardened wax, a
temple of vital gases, water with grass seed suspension,
glass blown through a cast of calcined gypsum, plaster of
Santo Spirito. Spiritous dissection, blood-sooty vapors,
the dense dance of the Renaissance counts down a Galenic
pulse. *Musculo vivicare.* Transit the venous. Bypass the
arterial. Underscore the two-part cantus firmus in heat
and motion.

(The fixed heart burns slow, spurns fervor.)

Little Song

Both guitars run trebly. One noodles
Over a groove. The other slushes chords.
Then they switch. It's quite an earnest affair.
They close my eyes. I close their eyes. A horn
Blares its inner air to brass. A girl shakes
Her ass. Some dude does the same. The music's
Gone moot. Who doesn't love it when the bass
Doesn't hide? When you can feel the trumpet peel
Old oil and spit from deep down the empty
Pit of a note or none or few? So don't
Give up on it yet: the scenario.
You know that it's just as tired of you
As you are of it. Still, there's much more to it
Than that. It does not not get you quite wrong.

The Beatitudes of Malibu

I

Walking across the PCH, we looked
Up and saw, big as the butt of a pen,
Jupiter, fat with light and unheighted.
I looked back at the waiting traffic stalled
At the seaside road's salt-rimmed traffic lights
As they swayed to the Pacific's not-quite-
Anapestic song of sea and air —
The raw and sudden crick of crickets —
The cars, suddenly silent as cows —
And blue Malibu blackening like a bee.

II

A poem is a view of the Pacific
And the Pacific, and the Pacific
Taking in its view of the Pacific,
And the Pacific as the Pacific
(Just like that: as though there's no Pacific)
Ends. A poem is the palm of the ocean,
Closing. It or she or he is merely,
Which means it or she or he is a mar.
But a mar made up of temperament and
Tempo — the red weather in the heart.

III

I'm about to get this all wrong, I know:
Santa Monica behind me, the ocean
To my left, Jupiter high above me,
And Malibu somewhere in my mind, flecked
With mist and dusk and Dylan and strange grays

In the sunsets that stripe the seaside hills
Like the tricolor of a country made
Of beauty, the dream of beauty, and smog.
Sadly, in my mind it's always snowing;
Which is beautiful but austere, unlike here.

IV

Along the thin pedestrian passage
Beside the PCH, just off Sunset,
Mel Gibson chants of beginnings and ends
And lies and facts — Jews and Blacks being
Both the lies and facts. His face is ruddy
Like bruschetta. He storms at the police
Because fuck them. He's wearing his T-shirt
Like a toga. He schools them his toga
Wisdom from toga times. He offers them
His toga. They offer him a ride — .

V

Arun's car carried us like metaphor
In a poem or painting; moving meaning;
Moving the current; being the current;
The terse tug of tides: still the great glamour;
Still, even as we speed on the 110,
The music in my head, the Jupiter
Of the mind's unstemmed Pacific Ocean
As it unfurls in the vapor trail of
Malibu, fragrant in far-off fluorescents,
Like a nocturnal flower calling you.

VI

Then, Downtown LA and LA Live surged
Up, like marginalia on a newly
Turned page, spangled with bland suggestions,
Fiery accusations of its own
Brilliance that descend into indifference.
We speed nearer and it grows. We veer and
It grows. We park and it grows. Close your eyes.
Now look. And it has grown. Yo la quiero.
But I should know better, if just because
You can smell the injustice in the air.

VII

The Pacific encircles me. Slowly.
As though it doesn't trust me. Or, better
Said, I only understand it this way:
By feeling like a stranger at its blue
Door. The poet with the sea stuck in his
Enjambments can't call out to some Cathay
As though some Cathay exists and be glad.
No, the differences we have should be felt
And made, through that feeling, an eclipsed lack;
A power to take in what you can't take back.

VIII

The old hocus of this ocean's focus
On pulling its waves over the soft surf
Like a skin pulled down tight over the top
Of a drum was, to her, a new hocus.
We stared out with her, out toward Hokusai's

Tiny boats and rising lace-fringed sea swells
No chunk of haiku could think to charter.
It was like the eighth day of creation
In the eighth line of a poem — she sang,
She didn't sing, the sea sang, then stopped.

JOHN KOETHE

A Private Singularity

I used to like being young, and I still do,
Because I think I still am. There are physical
Objections to that thought, and yet what
Fascinates me now is how obsessed I was at thirty-five
With feeling older than I was: it seemed so smart
And worldly, so fastidiously knowing to dwell so much
On time — on what it gives, what it destroys, on how it feels.
And now it's here and doesn't feel like anything at all:
A little warm perhaps, a little cool, but mostly waiting on my
Life to fill it up, and meanwhile living in the light and listening
To the music floating through my living room each night.
It's something you can only recognize in retrospect, long after
Everything that used to fill those years has disappeared
And they've become regrets and images, leaving you alone
In a perpetual present, in a nondescript small room where it began.
You find it in yourself: the ways that led inexorably from
Home to here are simply stories now, leading nowhere anymore;
The wilderness they led through is the space behind a door
Through which a sentence flows, following a map in the heart.
Along the way the self that you were born with turns into
The self that you created, but they come together at the end,
United in the memory where time began: the tinkling of a bell
On a garden gate in Combray, or the clang of a driven nail
In a Los Angeles backyard, or a pure, angelic clang in Nova Scotia —
Whatever age restores. It isn't the generalizations that I loved
At thirty-five that move me now, but particular moments
When my life comes into focus, and the feeling of the years
Between them comes alive. Time stops, and then resumes its story,
Like a train to Balbec or a steamer to Brazil. We moved to San Diego,
Then I headed east, then settled in the middle of the country
Where I've waited now for almost forty years, going through the
Motions of the moments as they pass from now to nothing,
Reading by their light. I don't know why I'm reading them again —
Elizabeth Bishop, Proust. The stories you remember feel like mirrors,
And rereading them like leafing through your life at a certain age,

As though the years were pages. I keep living in the light
Under the door, waiting on those vague sensations floating in
And out of consciousness like odors, like the smell of sperm and lilacs.
In the afternoon I bicycle to a park that overlooks Lake Michigan,
Linger on a bench and read *Contre Sainte-Beuve* and *Time Reborn*,
A physics book that argues time is real. And that's my life —
It isn't much, and yet it hangs together: its obsessions dovetail
With each other, as the private world of my experience takes its place
Within a natural order that absorbs it, but for a while lets it live.
It feels like such a miracle, this life: it promises everything,
And even keeps its promise when you've grown too old to care.
It seems unremarkable at first, and then as time goes by it
Starts to seem unreal, a figment of the years inside a universe
That flows around them and dissolves them in the end,
But meanwhile lets you linger in a universe of one —
A village on a summer afternoon, a garden after dark,
A small backyard beneath a boring California sky.
I said I still felt young, and so I am, yet what that means
Eludes me. Maybe it's the feeling of the presence
Of the past, or of its disappearance, or both of them at once —
A long estrangement and a private singularity, intact
Within a tinkling bell, an iron nail, a pure, angelic clang —
The echo of a clear, metallic sound from childhood,
Where time began: "Oh, beautiful sound, strike again!"

FRANCINE J. HARRIS

enough food and a mom

The dad. body has just enough gravy on his plate
   to sop up one piece of bread. So, enough for one
   supper, says the mom. She comes back to him, says
don't argue with mom, you're a ghost. There's enough
   water around to drown a cob in its husk. in a dad. He puts
up weather stripping all night. to keep out the mom. He says

I should have cooked for you more. She thinks she could
   make her own insulin. to keep from going into dad.
She says I should have married a ghost. says: You have a
little raisin on your lip. a little. The mom says
   stop all that quiet, it's foolish.
   Come on now, dad. come to ghost.

says the ghost.

I won't even warn the mom. I won't even flinch if the ghost
   tries to hold her mom. After all,
a good séance starts with enough food
   and a mom. The ghost with a biscuit in meat. The mom
with the smell of cracked dad. sucked out of oxygen.
   The mom is a smell of wrecked vines.

     You, the dad. with no teeth. And no, (the mom)
is a garden full of ghost. No. says the dad: lost in ashes.

No city is complete. its own worst ghost. who can't
   remember the ghost now, the ghost says:
   All your selves know, now.
They ghost like the bushel of a snowflower.

Everyone is dead. now. says, the ghost.
   The mom is a yard of blackening petals.

At night, I have really long dads. Without the ghosts,
    I wake in a puddle of ghost.
        But you'll be mom one day. to know I am alive.
We are all sappy dad, aren't we. Tell the ghost, it's ok.
        Let the bodies lie ghost for a while.

    I mom of you. I mom of you a lot.

Venus

Death is coming
and you must build a starship
to take you to Venus.

Make it from a catsup bottle,
a flashlight coil,
a penny, the cat's bell,
Mom's charm bracelet.

They say that planet is torment,
whipped by circular wind,
choked in vitriol clouds.

But no. When you get there
it is a light in the sky
and I am with you.

If you find nothing else,
borrow the pleated wing
of a winter moth,
lighter than dust.

ALLI WARREN

I Want to Thank the Wind Blows

Sound of the rain so I know
there's constraint
sound of the train
so I know commerce
has not come to a standstill
now they raise the barrier
now they set it back in place

What coats the bottom
of the surface of the sound
when the swifts come in
when the clerks come home
who will bathe the children
who will bake the bread

when the luff is tight
when the mainsheet
starts the boat underway

whatever you do don't
let the tongue slip
from its moorings

what's that song?
love lift us up where we belong

I ate the pill
and the pill was real

There's Always Some Bird Dog

Guards demand we waltz
the teeming hedge
soldiers spread
but can't quell
what wells

worthwhile's a made shape
wafting about
in the night so green
all bright ornament
and creamy delay

I take off my hat
I get off and walk

O skin be strong
expand rewardable range
build steady wealth
of shared play
don't end at lending
nouns to property

consult the ear
consult the air

claim common right
to lick up excess
as a lock's for frisking
a gale's gaping gate

they say the submarine
which waves no flag
is a violator vessel

how soft its coax
how smooth its thick white head

so maybe it matters
who claims cause
of that couplet

adorned and anointed
the bodies of my loves
the fear grins
of great apes

ARTHUR VOGELSANG

Extinct

If you give money to an animal
He or she gets cloying and aggressive
But when arrested for that behavior
Says, "I didn't know anything, my reps
Did it. Well they did. These humans
Committed their tiny crimes in the mail," it says,
"Knowing animals are photogenic. You can hold
One in your lap or hold a sheaf of photos
In which a feline looks like you yourself tearing off a leg
Of a springbok antelope, which prey looks like you
Concentrating on the flee instinct," it says.
I tend to agree with it. It and
All of them have expressions on their faces, four limbs,
Two eyes, noses, ears, etcetera, how close can you get to you
Or me, and then there's the same insides. If it is a cheetah
Do not put it in your lap. If it's
A black rhino it weighs 2,250 lbs.
And has *two*! sharp horns about 24 in. ea.!
Let's suppose nothing about that one and not say
It has a facial expression. My own opinion
Is it will have one in a matter of time.
There are ten other scenes in which I look like the animals
In them so don't argue I'm writing yet another check this week
And as a matter of fact I'd like to smack something,
Bite it, and cook it. You do that, tonight
For instance. If one of us eats the other
It's a very big crime
Not tiny like the revolutionary revelation in a solicitation
That we are like the animals, no, *are* them,
Which is bigger in evolution and spirituality,
Sure, and in the final accounting
Much more important, but today
Don't put a cheetah in your lap and don't eat other humans.

ROBERT FERNANDEZ

Now the Slow Blood

Slow the voice goes slower.
Slow the slow rain down.
Slow the narrow fellow in the grass stiffens.
Now the slow blood stirs.
Slow the voice goes slower:
Soft lead, soft enough to eat.
We dine on soft lead with lampreys.
Slow the voice goes down to harden.
Slow the silt reaches the bottom,
And Davy Jones eats
His slow meal of rubber and clay.
Slow the slow rain down can rain.
Slow the dead is dead.
Slow the light, light.
Slow the spirit is a bone,
Toy from a child's coffin.

Tragedy

Melt the fat around the heart;
Leave only muscle.

For us
Spectators

Leave
Only muscle;

Only trim the fat
To depth.

And, even if you
Nick the heart,

If you tear it
Or scratch it,

If you slice a petal off it,
Don't sweat it.

Be mindful only
That you leave the muscle

Clean,
Sheared of fat.

Or you can
Char the heart,

Melt down the fat,
Then eat it

With fucking
Fava beans.

Whatever you do,
Be sure

To leave the heart
Muscled: thick and delicious.

For we, citizens, have come
To both see and to be

The god and the heart;
We have come to become

The horns of the heart
Splintered into

Their plumpest sections.

DANA LEVIN

The Living Teaching

You wanted to be a butcher
but they made you be a lawyer.

You brought home presents
when it was nobody's birthday.

Smashed platters of meat
she cut against the grain.

Were a kind
of portable shrine —

I was supposed to cultivate a field of bliss,
then return to my ordinary mind.

You burned the files
and moved the office.

Made your children fear
a different school.

Liked your butter hard
and your candy frozen.

Were a kind
of diamond drill, drilling a hole
right through my skull —

quality sleep, late November.

What did it mean, "field of bliss" —

A sky alive "with your greatest mentor" —

I wore your shoes, big as boats,
       flopped through the house —
       while you made garlic eggs with garlic salt, what

       "represents the living teaching" —

Sausages on toasted rye with a pickle,
and a smother of cheese, and
frosting
       right out of the can without the cake —

You ruled
       with a knife in one hand and a fork in the other, you raged
       at my stony mother, while I banged

       from my high chair, waving
       the bloodied bone

       of something slaughtered — I was
       a butcher's daughter.

So all hail to me —

       Os Gurges, Vortex Mouth, I gap my craw
       and the bakeries of the cities fall, I

       stomp the docks — spew out a bullet stream
       of oyster shells, I'll

       drain the seas — the silos
       on every farm, the rice

       from the paddy fields, the fruit

from all the orchard trees, and then I'll

eat the trees —

I'll eat with money and I'll eat
with my teeth until the rocks

and the mountains curl
and my blood sings —

I'm such a good girl

to eat the world.

Banana Palace

I want you to know
how it felt to hold it,
        deep in the well of my eye.

You, future person: star of one of my
complicated dooms —

This one's called Back to the Dark.

Scene 1: Death stampedes through the server-cities.

Somehow we all end up living in caves, foraging in civic ruin.

Banana Palace — the last
        of the last of my kind who can read
        breathes it hot
                into your doom-rimed ear.

She's a dowser of spine-broken books and loose paper
        the rest of your famishing band thinks mad.

                •

Mine was the era
of spending your time
        in town squares made out of air.

You invented a face
        and moved it around, visited briefly
        with other faces.

        Thus we streamed
        down lit screens

        sharing pictures of animals looking ridiculous —

trading portals to shoes, love, songs, news, somebody's latest
		rabid cause: bosses, gluten, bacon, God —

Information about information was the pollen we
deposited —
		while in the real fields bees starved.

		Into this noise sailed
		Banana Palace.

					•

It was a mother ship of gold.

Shining out between HAPPY BDAY KATIE!
		and a photo of someone's broken toe —

Like luminous pillows cocked on a hinge,
like a house
		with a heavy lid, a round house of platelets and honey —

It was open,
		like a box that holds a ring.

		And inside, where the ring would be:

					•

I think about you a lot, future person.

How you will need
all the books that were ever read
		when the screens and wires go dumb.

Whatever you haven't used
        for kindling or bedding.

Whatever made it through
        the fuckcluster of bombs
        we launched accidentally,

            at the end of the era of feeling like no one
            was doing a thing

            about our complicated dooms —

Helpless and braced we sat in dark spaces

submerged in pools of projected images,
        trying to disappear into light —

            Light! There was so much light!
            It was hard to sleep.

                    •

Anyway.

Banana Palace.

Even now when I say it, cymbals
        shiver out in spheres. It starts to turn its
        yellow gears

        and opens like a clam. Revealing

            a fetal curl on its temple floor,
                    bagged and sleeping —

a white cocoon

under lit strings that stretch
     from floor to ceiling —

a harp made of glass

incubating
a covered

   •

    pearl —

We broke the world
you're living in,
    future person.

Maybe
that was always our end:
    to break the jungles to get at the sugar, leave behind
    a waste of cane —

There came a time
I couldn't look at trees without
    feeling elegiac — as if nature

    were already *over*,
      if you know what I mean.

It was the most glorious thing I had ever seen.

Cross-section of a banana under a microscope
    the caption read.

I hunched around my little screen
sharing a fruit no one could eat.

SUSAN BARBA

Seeking Even the Smallest of Signs

First they pulled from the burning a miracle, then a mistake.
The Lord will lift them the priest with the grief
in his eyes cried. Lord, what blue eyes bound there,
what hurling, diving, shining, burning—
reason surfaces and sinks, sinks and surfaces.

Dawn without sunrise. Gray. Purple.
Her Majesty in mourning. Her Majesty the warring. In the double
house of life all this was repeating itself,
Naneferkaptah had already himself lived Setne's story.

When the rains began the teams with two-by-fours
found the going treacherous as those in the desert found
the food wretched. They prayed to the golden serpent on the staff
to save them. And the serpent stretched itself
      tap, tap
and became a hymn, white-throated, rising to give
itself up for the good of the chosen ones.

      Mother I remember the buttons on your dressing gown.
      So blue and beady-eyed and true, when did I begin

To fear them. The world now
not so round with us. Velocity
threatening to meet, to marry
density at every corner
      carrying
      carrying

Who can see
      the writing on our foreheads almost wet still
Who can see
      tap, tap

algae bloom beneath the board
smoke from the sky

Tell me if that is a hand
if it is human what
will it
speak

STEPHEN SANDY

Governor's Place

The great house birch with its girth he never quite
could get his arms around, long felled, at last
only its bark like a larva's husk in grass
leaning neck-high, hollow below mansards.

He does not live in the peeling mansion, but
a more-than-ample keeper's cottage beyond
rolled lawns and relics of Victorian elms
where he muses in his study alcove. Touches
the ancient coins, silver or bronze, their gleam
on the baize-topped writing table — proud Athena
helmeted; her owl agog beneath. Eternity
glimpsed in the boy ruler Gordian's profile,
copper green.
                        Trees on guard in browed
dignity now the seething barrack of bees.
Nearby a maple twisted by wind for decades
spirals, a stair winding above the cone
of shade. In his covert the son, reading Herodotus,
Suetonius — staggering run of drachmas,
staters, tetradrachms, glinting in rows.

Modest Proposals

A longish poem about wallpaper.
A short lyric about discouragement in white.
A medium-length thesis of uncertain importance.
Another sonnet, about scholarship.
A couplet of olives.

A long narrative about the exaggeration of your absence.
Several quatrains about candle stubs.
That old sestina on Isaiah.
Palindromes about Scots presbyters of the 18th century.
Some rock lyrics from Benares.

A nature poem about committees.
Seven heroic couplets about Art Murphy.
Several more heroic couplets on Murphy's Law.
A ballad about studying Latin in Latium.
A masque for Mercedes and her Benz.

For Fresno's Best Process Service Call Hermes

True, my office is a gold Camino nineteen eighty-two
   & front-work's on a laptop, but there are older tricks:

this knack I have to spy a sham address: figures
   pried off siding or the silhouette that's left

when eight is changed to three; my talent to discern
   the perp who hides behind the car or ducks among

the bins or sidles, slams the screen & tries
   for silence then behind his gutted door. Some

will wave a gun or summon dogs. Once a rooster.
   Once an alderman who menaced with a mallet

(croquet) when his trucking company was sued
   & there's still this lucent bruise on my right heel —

long story: swan shot, tree house, veteran. Though
   no one wants this dachshund's weight of paper

compiled by some paralegal underpaid in Phoenix,
   I assure you I will always serve. I am the envoy

(a ball cap hides my third eye). Put me in swift shoes
   or wings, at some cosmic door with only sky behind —

black-clad, the Prophet of Xerox, steadfast
   bearer of a clerk court's smeared truncated seal.

I know these streets: the houses boarded up,
   the other heralds driving slow on fractured blacktop;

the sidewalks' glass & fenders scattered; vacant quarter
   acres returning now to palm & pampas, trees of heaven.

I am waiting at the crossroads, here at your broken gate
where barbed acacias stoop to shade my trespass.

In Case of Complete Reversal

Born into each seed
is a small anti-seed
useful in case of some
complete reversal:
a tiny but powerful
kit for adapting it
to the unimaginable.
If we could crack the
fineness of the shell
we'd see the
bundled minuses
stacked as in a safe,
ready for use
if things don't
go well.

All Your Horses

Say when rain
cannot make
you more wet
or a certain
thought can't
deepen and yet
you think it again:
you have lost
count. A larger
amount is
no longer a
larger amount.
There has been
a collapse; perhaps
in the night.
Like a rupture
in water (which
can't rupture
of course). All
your horses
broken out with
all your horses.

NOAH WARREN

Barcelona: Implication

The Constellations *are a harmoniously composed series of 23 gouaches that*
Miró painted to escape the trauma of the war years.
— *The Joan Miró Foundation*

We've all gouached.
Haven't we? Pollock lashed
stretched canvas that was Nude.
Was said to call his Ruth prude
and he spat chew in a coffee can
and shat bloodily in the can.

When I was twenty I spent three
hours in a room with the Free-
Spirited Types moving from
one inviting orifice to the welcome
of another. I was lost in my wood,
savage and stern. But also I understood
that when it was later and I was wiser
I could never forgive Herr Pfizer.

My father said we've all got an East River.
He had a tenuous web of veins for a liver.
His loss. Literally. Mom's impatient art
was proved to be the most effective part
of her mothering: you should see her rich greens
well up in the power of the middle and grow lean
as they colonize the crusted edges.
My love for her is impregnable.

Pity Miró, moonblind, weary on the rocky coast
of Portugal, walking cliff paths and getting lost.
His quest for childish wonder has bent him
and riddled his skin before its time.
Put this together with that! Paint it yellow!
Murk the sky with banks of Periwinkle and Snow.

Gouache a widened eye low on the right,
so it can behold the left and the night.

Across from the Winter Palace

Do you remember when you began to travel?
It lent you this astonishing lens and you kept a journal
That rode in your breast pocket like a stone,
There you wrote "Limoges —" and "Altenkirchen";
And when you saw a *peasant*, kissed, or passed out —
Died for twenty seconds — in the heat on the hill above
Marseille you would rush out the notebook and make a note —
Sometimes just an x in the top right corner —
And ideally you would brood about that later.

Which led slowly to the dark hot bar
Where you enjoy a glass of beer across from the Winter Palace in
    summer.
In the rose-and-blue windows of the basilica
Today radiant burghers stood and learned Mercy in a circle
Around Stephen, recognized
By the pebble enthroned in his skull and the scarlet ooze.

While in your system the amphetamines progress.
The idea is they'll give you heart to haul yourself up and cross
The limestone plaza. And when at the gate of the place
You pay you can enter the Palace.

FREEDOM OF SHADOW

DOUGLAS KEARNEY

Introduction

Like the afflicted shadows of Dante's Inferno, *I, Blanche Bruce, am also a phantom of sorts. Yet, unlike those banished to eternal anguish, I am blessed with mercurial powers that enable me to traverse the boundaries of time, space, and the earthly realm as I please. When ideal conditions arise, I have been known to assume the identities of other artists and to infiltrate their imaginations.... Our primary objective is to transform matter into energy, to render material immaterial.*
— Terry Adkins, *from* Shadow of Freedom

Early in 2013, I started a granted collaboration with installation artist, musician, sculptor, etc. etc., Terry Adkins. Only a year later, Terry died of a heart attack. Following his passing, I chose to proceed and continue with work in tribute to his art and its impact on mine — but focused on remembering Terry's alter ego, a figure named "Blanche Bruce" (after the first black US senator elected to serve a full term). That work — an oratorio for voice and digital turntables — is called *Freedom of Shadow*. But that's not what you'll see here.

Terry was adamant that the text for *whatever* we ended up doing not be produced as a book. So, in that spirit, I do not present the entire libretto. Instead, I've included some remarks about process and ideas (preemptive ekphrasis?), first drafts from my journals alongside finals, excerpted correspondence, and work deeply influenced by our conversations yet not germane to the oratorio. They collect questions of interdisciplinarity vs. collaboration, side-eyes at modernism, skepticism of Afrofuturism, dogged attachment to bad ideas, working documentation, and the use of "nigger" as verb.

Freedom of Shadow records and transforms the material we actually managed to create in collaboration: our e-mails, conversations, and discussions of each other's work. It presents this discourse as antagonisms and accords, duets, and theatrical environments. The oratorio addresses Blanche Bruce and not Terry Adkins in the main because I can only memorialize our interstice of aesthetics and poetics. I never got to meet the man, though I came close once, before I knew who he was. Yet ever present since our first conversation are Terry's provocations. They set the polestar of this project. I am grateful for that light, though it blanches and it bruises.

Behavioral feeling
of performed
ethnicity

A Threat to
Modernism

These two notes from our first one-on-one phone conversation have served as mooring. Terry brought these. The left: "behavioral feeling of performed ethnicity," I've come to think of as a kind of super-imposed gaze. Perhaps it's a variation of W.E.B. Du Bois's "double consciousness," only the subject has ramped-up his/her ethnic difference in anticipation of the onlooker's attention to it. Say, you are, I don't know, buck dancing in a storefront window, looking at someone looking at you. Yet, you look through your own jigging reflection as you see your audience (which now includes you, performing). I tried to get at this passive and aggressive self-consciousness — I've figured it since with the sense that Terry had antipathy for it — in a piece called "(Ghostmaking) or Ideal Conditions."

The second note, "a threat to modernism," reminded me of a Lincoln Motor Company ad I'd made into my own white whale, described in an e-mail excerpted a few pages from here. I will add however, that considering *Poetry*'s historical nurturing of modernism, the proposition of shitting a bit in the temple was perversely enticing.

On the spread after this: the first and then final draft of a number called "CAMH (On Sight)" — in 2012 I actually saw Terry perform at Contemporary Arts Museum Houston. I didn't realize this until several months after we began our collaboration.

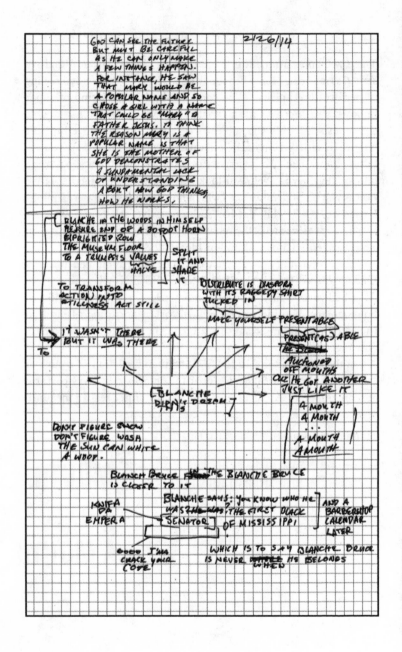

GOD CAN SEE THE FUTURE
BUT MUST BE CAREFUL
AS HE CAN ONLY MAKE
A FEW THINGS HAPPEN.
FOR INSTANCE, HE SAW
THAT MARY WOULD BE
A POPULAR NAME AND SO
CHOSE A GIRL WITH A NAME
THAT COULD BE "MARY" TO
FATHER JESUS. TO THINK
THE REASON MARY IS A
POPULAR NAME IS THAT
SHE IS THE MOTHER OF
GOD DEMONSTRATES
A FUNDAMENTAL LACK
OF UNDERSTANDING
ABOUT HOW GOD THINKS,
HOW HE WORKS.

2/26/14

BLANCHE IN THE WOODS IS HIMSELF
PLEASURE END OF A 30 FOOT HORN
ELPRIGHTED ROW
THE MUSEUM FLOOR
TO A TRUMPET'S VALVES

SPLIT
IT AND
SHADE
IT

HALVE

TO TRANSFORM
ACTION INTO
STILLNESS ACT STILL

DISTRIBUTE IS DIASPORA
WITH ITS RAGGEDY SHIRT
TUCKED IN

MAKE YOURSELF PRESENTABLE

IT WASN'T THERE
BUT IT WAS THERE

TO

PRESENT(4S) ABLE

THE

AUCTIONED
OFF MOUTHS
CUZ HE GOT ANOTHER
JUST LIKE IT

BLANCHE
DIDN'T DREAM

A MOUTH
A MOUTH
...
A MOUTH
A MOUTH

DON'T FIGURE SNOW
DON'T FIGURE WASH
THE SUN CAN WHITE
A WOOF.

BLANCH BRUCE THE BLANCHE BRUCE
IS CLOSER TO IT

KNIFA
DA
EMPERA

BLANCHE SAYS: YOU KNOW WHO HE
WAS? HE WAS THE FIRST BLACK
SENATOR OF MISSISSIPPI

AND A
BARBERSHOP
CALENDAR
LATER

GOOD JWA
CHECK YOUR
COTE

WHICH IS TO SAY BLANCHE BRUCE
IS NEVER WHERE HE BELONGS
WHEN

CAMH (On Sight)

[BLANCHE is in Houston
at the pleasure end of a salvo
of 18-foot horns,
erected row valves
the gallery floor
to a laminate trumpet.
this takes a long time
and we wonder. we shuffle]

} this halves, the gallery.
doles out.
doling is diaspora with its raggedy shirt tails tucked in.

TO TRANSFORM ACTION
INTO STILLNESS CAN'T ONE make yourself presentable
ACT STILL? [present (as) able]. blacks won't do
if they won't do.
[BLANCHE and his black band is sans
blat. a loud-assed blanched silence?
this takes a long time
and we wonder. we shuffle]

RE: ETYMOLOGIES
& CAUSATIONS
don't figure snow
don't figure wash
the sun can white a wood.

[BLANCHE has auctioned off
mouths because he got another
[BLANCHE BRUCE in the BLANCHE BRUCE just like them]
is closer to it. RE: BLANCHE in the woods.]
you know who he was the first
black senator to full and of Mississippi.
[this is just to say BLANCHE BRUCE is never
when he belongs.
I'm sorry.]   TO BLANCHE IN THE WOODS IS
TO BE SPOOKED AMONG TALL,
OLD THINGS. "We all share
a common af-
finity for the
intrinsic   re-
ward of col-
laborative con-
sciousness…"

th'hell's gon happen with
them horns?

A MOUTH.

A MOUTH.

…A MOUTH.

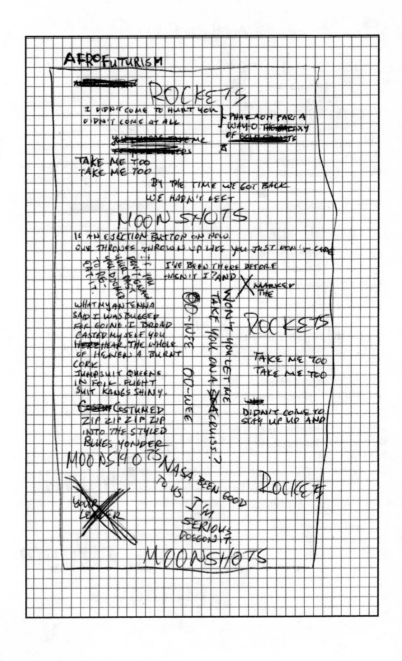

Afrofuturism (Blanche says, "Meh")

After Lauren Halsey and Mike Demps

won't you let me take you on a ~~red~~ cruise?

ROCKETS

so far ahead
it's behind us.
Moses tote her
raygun saying
moonwalk or git
disinigrated!

TAKE ME TO ~~YOUR LEADER~~
TAKE ME TO ~~YOUR LEADER~~
TAKE ME TO ~~YOUR LEADER~~
TAKE ME TO ~~YOUR LEADER~~
TAKE ME TO ~~YOUR LEADER~~
TAKE ME TO ~~YOUR LEADER~~
TAKE ME TO ~~YOUR LEADER~~
TAKE ME TO ~~YOUR LEADER~~
TAKE ME TO ~~YOUR LEADER~~
TAKE ME TO ~~YOUR LEADER~~
TAKE ME TO ~~YOUR LEADER~~
TAKE ME TO ~~YOUR LEADER~~
TAKE ME TO ~~YOUR LEADER~~
TAKE ME TO ~~YOUR LEADER~~
TAKE ME TO ~~YOUR LEADER~~
TAKE ME TO ~~YOUR LEADER~~

pharaohs go far away-o, no rid-ing place down dere!

thrones thrown up like they just don't care!

[elect]

MOONSHOTS

what our antenna said we was bugged,
so us eyed the light up to light out.
whole of "…the place" blacked up so blacks out
this terra. o great gettin up launchin!
spacesuited Q.U.E.E.N.S. in foil to fly.
flightsuited kings sky around shinin.
zip zip zip off the planetation,
beyond the stairs to nigga heaven.

ROCKETS

IT'S AN ESCAPE CRAFT
FROM NOW&THEN
BY WAY OF THEN&SOON.

"yeahyeahyeahyeah"
"yeahyeahyeahyeah"

MOONSHOTS

who you callin BUCK Rogers?"

it's the Where,
the When we go
when the Call
gets no Response.
[do you read?
over.]

ASTROSHEEN®
REMY MARTIAN®
~~CADILLITE®~~
~~CADILLAC®~~ ~~GALACTIC®~~
SPACEY ADAMS®

TAKE ME TO ~~YOUR LEADER~~
TAKE ME TO ~~YOUR LEADER~~
TAKE ME TO ~~YOUR LEADER~~
TAKE ME TO ~~YOUR LEADER~~
TAKE ME TO ~~YOUR LEADER~~

ROCKETS

"NASA been good to us!
Dogonnit, I'm serious!"

"pilot…
"pilot…
"pilot…
"pilot…
"pilot…

are we *there* yet?
are we *we* yet?
are we *we* there?
are there *we* there yet?
are we here *yet* there?
there,   there.

ooo-zweee!

MOONSHOTS

who you callin StarBUCK?"

~~THE SOUND CITY~~

{ A LADDER THAT
{ CLINGS LOW.
MY ~~DESCENT DEST~~

MY ~~DESET~~

MY DECENT DESCENT TO DISSENT
I WAS THERE WHEN THEY
YOU GOT NOTHING ON ME

I ~~AM~~

I'M AWAITING THE
VARIATION DEMANDED.

THE AFROFUTURIST
OPERAS

1. PILOT
2. ~~BIG~~ SKINS
3. BOX
4. A~~CITY~~
5 TAR CITY
6. GHOST CITY
7. RED CITY
8. BLOCK
9. SEENT
10. HOOD

AUTOMATIC SLIM
RAZOR TOTING JIM
BUTCHER KNIFE TOT
FAST TALKIN FA

...

COOTER CRAWLIN
ABYSSINIA RED
PISTOL PETE

'11
FATS
WASHBOARD SAM
SHAKIN BOXCA
PEGGY CAROLIN
PEG ~~~~
CAROLINE DYE

13

From the outset, I'd set out to propose opera to Terry. It was a shot of his *Darkwater* installation — which spoked around an obelisk of kick drums (*Muffled Drums*) — that spoke to me immediately. I wondered what world demanded architecture resembling an acoustic sound system. What soundclash in what yard.

Additionally, I had seen photos of Terry playing what looks like a soprano sax while decked in a shaggy, Sanford Biggers-designed suit and began to imagine what a performance would look like with him all Ghetto Birded-down. What narrative would ground that image.

I was prepping to suggest ten two-page operas like *Jig*, which I published in the chapbook, *SkinMag*. Actually started on *Skin* and *Seent* before chucking them back in the kettle. I would abandon the opera idea and several others before returning to it.

Plus! At bottom-right, you'll see the list of party guests from Koko Taylor's "Wang Dang Doodle." An unrelated seed for a series.

Also kettled.

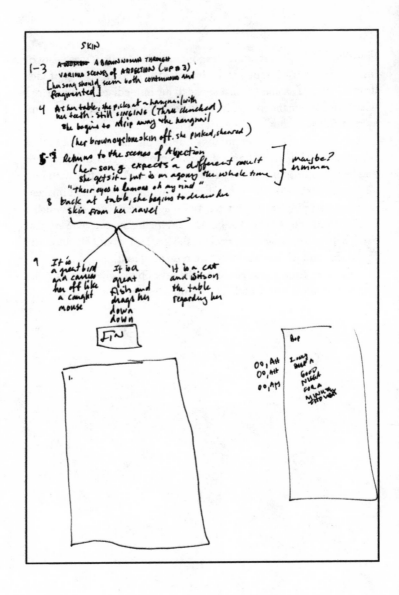

SKIN

1-3 A WOMAN A BROWN WOMAN THROUGH
     VARIOUS SCENES of ABJECTION (LUP # 3)
     [her song should seem both continuous and
     fragmented]

4 At her table, she picks at a hangnail (with
   her teeth. Still SINGING (Thru clenched)
   she begins to strip away the hangnail
        (her brown eyelone skin off. she pinked, sheared)

5-7 Returns to the scenes of Abjection
     (her son & expects a different result] maybe?
     she gets it — but is in agony the whole time } unman
     "their eyes is lemons oh my rind"
8 back at table, she begins to draw her
   skin from her navel

9 It is
   a great bird   It is a   It is a cat
   and carries   great   and sits on
   her off like   fish and   the table
   a caught   drags her   regarding her
   mouse   down
                         down

FIN

1.

B4P
OO, AH   I OWE
OO, AH   BUT A
OO, AH   GOOD
            NIGHT
            FOR A
            MINUTE
            THO WORK

Skin was one of the two-page operas. When I was developing this, I hadn't gotten my mind right for collaboration.

Terry was interested in opera as an idea—but when he asked me where he fit in, I imagined his existing work served as world-building prompts. I would write *into* his installations, repurposing his sculptures as set pieces and even characters, then, he would create production-style sketches to flesh out the speculative production. Performance would be me on vox and maybe some electric drum patterns (beats, beats, beats), and him on horns.

This wasn't a terribly compelling way of working together. Our processes wouldn't be challenged enough by the arrangement. I would essentially be writing ekphrastic poetry, a fine thing, but I find myself arguing that when a poet not only responds to an artist's work, but is in dialogue about new work with said artist, ekphrasis seems inadequate. A kind of lyric stenography of meeting minutes. Why write a dialogue between the poem and the object (collaboration) when they can be fused, interwoven?

The trouble with the way I think of interdisciplinarity—one art form synthesizing another art form—is that it might obviate the need for multiple artists. If you can write, I don't know, a rhetorical butoh, including kinetic butoh may just be redundant.

I found myself stuck. Either I would go ahead and draft, fixing Terry in the role of production artist, or write a kind of preemptive ekphrasis, an ekphrasis for art yet to be (and possibly never to be) created. A fantastic prompt for a solitary writer, but a thorny strategy for collaboration, I suspect.

4/26/14

THAT LOUD-ASSED COLORED
SILENCE: ~~xxxxxxxx~~
MODERNITY PART 2

~~SHATTERSB HAMMER~~
~~xxxxxxx~~
HAMMER SHATTERED
NAIL ~~NAIL~~
SHATTERED ~~xxxxxxx~~ PLANK
~~PLANK~~ SHATTERED ROOF
~~ROOF~~ SHATTERED HOUSE
~~HOUSE~~ SHATTERED COUPLE
~~COUPLE~~ SHATTERED ~~xxxx~~ EYES
~~6 EYES~~ SHATTERED CULM
~~CULM~~ ~~xxxxxxxxxxxxx~~
~~xxxxxxxxxxxxxxx~~ BECAUSE, YOU SEE:
THE ~~xxx~~ TOOL DON'T WORK HA HA
HA HA HA HA HA HA HA HA HA HA HA
HA HA HA HA HA HA HA HA HA
Go Long TOOLEY!

1. TO NIGGER A THING
   IS NOT A SILENCING
   BUT VOICING.
2. THE NIGGER HAS NO
   PLACE IN A LOUD-ASSED
   COLORED SILENCE.
3. THE NEGRO HAS A SMALL PLOT
   THERE
4. A KIND OF KITCHENETTE THERE
   KIND OF COLORLESS EYE AND
   PHLEGMATIC COFFEE POT
5. THE NIGRA HAS A PLACE ADJACENT
   TO LOUD-ASSED COLORED SILENCE,
   AS THE NIGRA FILES
6. DISCERN BETWEEN NEGRO AND NIGRA
   BY THE ~~xxxx~~ FORM OF ITS CLAVICLE.
   THE NIGRA'S IS YOKE LIKE, THE NEGRO'S
   LIKE A BOW
7. BOTH ~~xx~~ MOST AT HOME IN THE LOUD-
   ASSED COLORED SILENCE IS THE BLACK.
8. INKSKIRTED THERE A COLONIAL SPREAD.
9. EVERY ROOM BOASTS A TRAP DRUM.
10. EVERY ROOM BOASTS A STEREO
11. EVERY ROOM BOASTS A TRUMPET
12. THERE ARE MUTES FOR EVERYTHING.
13. DON'T YOU ROLL THEM EYES.
14. DON'T YOU ROLL THEM EYES.
15. YOU MIGHT CONSTRUE THAT TO BLACK
    A THING IS TO SILENT IT.
16. DON'T YOU ROLL THEM EYES
17. BUT TO BLACK A THING IS SIMPLY NOT
    TO LISTEN TO IT.
18. I
19. SOMETHING FALLS?

That Loud-Assed Colored Silence: Modernity #2

shattered hammer hammers shattered
nail nails shattered plank planks
shattered roof roofs shattered
house houses shattered couple
couples shattered sex sexes shattered
pleasure pleasures shattered cum cums
shattered face gets shattered

BECAUSE, YOU SEE:
THE TOOL DON'T WORK!

HA! HA! HA! HA! HA! HA! HA! HA! HA! HA! HA! HA! HA! HA!
HA! HA! HA! HA! HA! HA! HA! HA! HA! HA! HA! HA! HA!

GO LONG, TOOLEY!

1. to nigger a thing's not silencing,
   rather voicing.
2. the niggered has no place
   in a loud-assed colored silence.
3. negro keeps a modest plot there.
4. a kind of kitchenette there
   kind of coiled red eye under brewer.
5. nigra lives adjacent
   to loud-assed colored silence.
6. not far, as the nigra flies.
7. discern between negro and nigra
   by the shape of their clavicles.
8. resembles a yoke? nigra.
   resembles a coat hanger? negro.
9. the black has the most place
   in a loud-assed colored silence.
10. inherited there a colonial manse.
11. in each room: trap drum set.
12. in each room: trumpet.
13. in each room: stereoo.
14. for everything: mutes.
15. don't you roll them eyes.
16. don't you roll them eyes.
17. you might construe
    to black a thing's silencing.
18. incorrect.
19. don't you roll them eyes.
20. to black a thing's
    to stop listening
    to it.
21.
22.
23.
24. something falls (?)

Sent October 8, 2013

Hello Terry,

... I do have a couple of more concrete ideas.

The first: I get that you are less interested in interrogating images. Remember that piece I sent, "That Loud-Assed Colored Silence"? That's something I've been thinking about as a kind of vector of primarily music criticism doubling as a comment about the erasure of black presence (which isn't strictly visual). It combines stuff I've read about jazz (particularly instrumental jazz) and reactions against the black (usu. male) voice in early hip hop, along with the celebration of the contemporary beat music scene (which also often gets rid of the voice). I am ambivalent about a lot of this stuff, but deeply intrigued by what the presence/absence is. Because of course I know that the "voiced" trumpet or dusty breakbeat are still black voices — cyborgish perhaps but certainly fugitive as Moten writes. But there's an intraracial class thing there as well.

Your drum tower and other metonymic pieces seem particularly interesting to me. On one level, sure, they could act as landscapes for the sonic fictions Kodwo Eshun talks about. But I also appreciate how they signify even with their absences and abstracting (not necessarily abstraction).

Since you mentioned illustrating short poems (both of my ideas approach this strategy), perhaps you might imagine the erasure/obfuscation of black subjects/signifiers/presence from sonic contexts and render those? I think there's a modernist critique possible there. How black folks are modern if they're cool and NOT talking? Have you seen the Lincoln commercial where they have a suited black man in a car factory playing drums (:31) all among that robotic new labor? Ain't he free? That shit is romantic modernism, nostalgia, even as it comes in a fragmented anachronistic image-filled commercial. Anyway, that's one.

The second is a little more episodic, but because we have a quicker publication timeline, it could be interesting. These would be shorter pieces, a la Harryette Mullen prose poems that are short bits of media criticism — contemporary stuff, ripped from the headlines. Twerking, Twix commercials, zombie obsessions, urban dance films. These could also be illustrated.

Thoughts,
DK

On October 11, 2013, Terry shot me a PDF via email, excerpted here:

Funny you should mention visible/invisible. Please find attached a book that just went to press in Ravenna, Italy by my alter ego döppelganger Blanche Bruce, named after the first Black senator to serve a full term. He represented Mississippi after Reconstruction. Give it a read and you'll see that we're on the same page. Perhaps photography is a more viable alternative than sculpture ... Still want to do the live thing too ...

The book, *Shadow of Freedom*, collects a number of photographs, many featuring Terry Adkins as Blanche Bruce — black-cloaked and capped — in what seems a freeze-dried landscape. He leaps a rut into a field. He stands in a doorway. Even in images without him, I thought I saw him, over there in the cut. The architecture's crooked shadow the same angular shape of his cape, a barn door ajar, scrub pipping hard land, there, yes? There? Haunting it all. Most importantly, the book contains an essay Terry wrote from the Blanche Bruce persona's point of view.

I mentioned earlier that Terry didn't want a book. Rather, he wanted a folio, a box full of papers, unbound, asequential. He had also mentioned, in a phone conversation, the generative power of a hoax, and even detailed one about George Washington Carver.

By the New Year, I had finally figured out what to do: document Blanche Bruce, perhaps forge accounts, surveillance reports, folksongs, clippings. A counterfeit dossier of sorts. I reckoned the poetic impulse would be at a macro-level — I would ask, in essence, whether the dossier were vehicle or tenor of Terry's aesthetics organized in the character of Blanche Bruce. Or, perhaps, it would be a philosophical/aesthetic process of engaging immaterial material (false documentation) to materialize the immaterial (a persona). I imagined that making this would require a series of interviews with Terry. He would become, I figured, the writer. I would become — through having to design a number of credible bits of ephemera, tear sheets from imagined glossies, etc. — the visual artist.

The live thing could be an oratorio, a narrative linking the dossier's collage. This was my last idea before moving into some word-and-picture jive. We had a soft deadline approaching and I wanted to nail this proposal, to make Terry excited about it. I planned to do a mock-up of several parts so I could show what I was talking about.

A couple of weeks later, Terry was gone.

Let us go then, let us go then,
~~streets~~ ~~shining~~
AND THE SPIT ~~IN THE HORN~~ SHINES THE
CHITLINS OF THE SAX. WET.
MAKE MUD OF DUST. MAKE
SOIL OF STONE. THE MUD
PEOPLE OF THE DIRT IS THAT
THE VEIN, THE SHRIMP SHIT
IN THE COLD PINE THE
DOORS TO THE ROOM BLOWN
OUT, THE OUT BLOWN IN,
Let us go then, let us go then,
THE SPIT'S TENEMENTS OF
BUBBLES, THE VORTEX
OF WIND AND WATER
CHECKMATE IN THE
PARK, NIGGA, CHECK
MATE, PAWN.
PREFERENCE FOR RED OR WHITE
PREFERENCE FOR Cold or Hot
It is because it's where it is
isn't it?
    But the shape, you see,
    is chewed up — I said
    But the shape, you see,
    is spit out — I said
I said we chased the color
out. I said we did it
with a stick. I said
~~Here's~~ HERE'S WHAT WE'LL DO.
AND IN A SHARP SKIN SUIT
GOT DOWN ON MY TRAP, A
FACTORY OF LIMBS AND I
SAID, WELL WHO KNOWS
WHO'LL BUY THESE. AND
I SAID, I'LL MAKE SOME
MORE. FUCK IT. SHOT
RIMS KICKED AND BRUSHED
I WAITED — THE WETNESS
CAME ON BRASS WITH A
GORILLA SUIT ON — THE
METONYM CAME ON —
I SAID CIV I UH II
UH III UH IV up to
XXII AND TOOK IT
TO THE BRIDGE

WET,
WET,
WET,
MOLD ON THE MARBLE
GAINING ON YOU — I
SAID GAINING ON
YOU. I SAID I'LL
TAKE MY TIME AND
YOURS. UH-I
UH II UH III
~~STARTED~~
THERE'S ONLY ONE
WAY, I SAID.
IN2

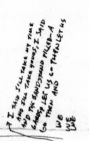

I SAID I'LL TAKE MY TIME
AND I'LL TAKE YOURS, I SAID
GAINING. LET US GO THEN LET US
GO THEN AND — THEN LET US
WE WE II

BLANCHE
BRUCE
DOES
THE
MODERNISM

LET US GO THEN, LET US GO THEN
I SAID. AND THE BAND
WAS I EVERY WHICH WAY.
THE SPIT SOAKED THE SAX'S
CHITLINS. I SAID THE WET
WOULD MAKE A MUD OF DUST,
A SOIL OF RED ROCK, I SAID.
THE DOORS TO THE ROOM BLOWN
OUT. THE OUT BLOWN IN,
LET US GO THEN, LET US GO THEN.
I SAID LOOK AT THE SPIT'S TENEMENTS
OF PHLEGM. I SAID LOOK AT ITS
SLOW TYPHOON. BLOOMING
THE ~~BRASS~~ UP. MAKES A LOAM OF
GYPSUM, I SAID, AN EARTH OF
MARBLE.
    PREFERENCE FOR RED OR WHITE?
    I ASKED, AND SWALLOWED MY SPIT,
WHERE I WAS WAS WHERE TO BE WHEN I WAS THIS
AND WHAT I MADE WAS BECAUSE IT WAS
WHERE IT ~~IS~~ WAS, WASN'T IT? I ASKED.
    BUT THE BODY ISN'T THERE, I SAID.
BUT THE SHAPES ~~ARE~~ ARE ~~ARE~~ THERE, I SAID.
    THE BODY WAS CHEWED UP AND SPAT OUT
    BY THE PERFECT SHAPES.
I SUGGESTED WE CHASE THE COLOR IN,
WITH A STICK, I SAID. HERE'S WHAT
WE'LL DO.
    LET US GO THEN, LET US GO THEN.
WHALING AND WAILING, TILL ONE WAS OVER
THE WALL, I SAID. IN A ~~FISH SKIN~~ SUIT
~~GOT DOWN~~ AND FREE ON MY TRAP, A FACTORY
OF LIMBS AND I SAID ~~WELL WHO KNOWS~~
~~WHO'LL BUY THIS~~ FUCK IT. ~~SHOT RIMS, KICKED~~
AND ~~BRUSHED AND~~ I WAITED IN A GORILLA
SUIT FOR THE WETNESS TO COME ON.
I SAID UH I UH II UH III UH ~~LXX~~ LXXIII
AND TOOK IT TO THE BRIDGE WET WET WET
MOLD ON THE MARBLE A ~~SUGAR~~ SALAD A CROP
~~EN~~ GAINING ON YOU I SAID GAINING ON YOU

Blanche Bruce Does the Modernism

let us go then let us go then I said

and the band was I lone every which
way way my spit slicked the sax's brass chitlins. I said

such wet would
mud dust and soil red rock. I said

doors to some room blown out the out
blown in. let us go then let us go then. I said

check the spit's phlegm
tenements. I said

its slow typhoon syrup. it blooms the axe up and
loams gypsum I said

earths marblebaster. let us go then let us go then I
said.

preference of red or white I said

my spit. where I was was where to
be when I was there and what I made was it since it was where it was
wasn't it I said.

but the body mustn't be there I said.

but the shapes are
there I said

here's what we'll do. let us go then let us go then wailing
and whaling till one was off the chain I said

fuck it. keeping time in a
gorilla suit for the mud to come on uh I uh II uh III ... uh CXVII and
took it to the bridge to throw down wet

wet

wet I said.

mold on that alabarble a salad
a crop gainin on yuh in a gorilla suit I said.

gaining on you I said

I'll take
my time and yours and the bandstand gardened out let us go then let
us go then and then we

we

we

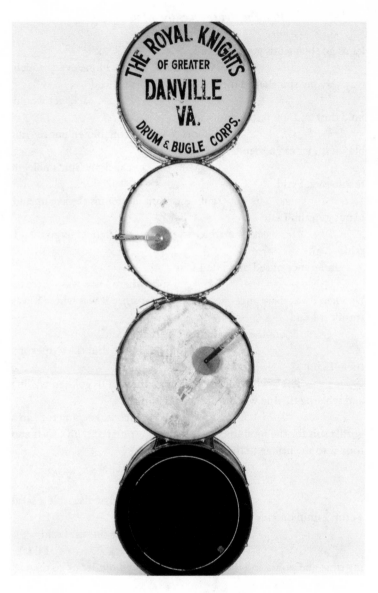

Terry Adkins, *Muffled Drums*, 2003–2013 (detail), bass drums, mufflers. Collection of Tate Modern. Image courtesy of the Estate of Terry Adkins and Salon 94, New York.

COMMENT

LESLEY WHEELER

Undead Eliot: How "The Waste Land" Sounds Now

When reading a poet who found his own voice after 1922, I often come across a cadence or trick of diction which makes me say "Oh, he's read Hardy, or Yeats, or Rilke," but seldom, if ever, can I detect an immediate, direct influence from Eliot. His indirect influence has, of course, been immense, but I should be hard put to it to say exactly what it is.
    — W.H. Auden

Thomas Sayers Ellis, or a version of him looping eternally on YouTube, is about to read "All Their Stanzas Look Alike," a weirdly hypnotic indictment of academic and aesthetic politics. Before launching into the poem, he remarks:

> I was beat digging at the artist's colony, it's kind of funny, and I heard "let us go then you and I when the evening is spread out against the sky in a red wheelbarrow and that has made all the difference." The cadence of that decade became my new haint, the new thing that haunted me, and so I wrote this — this is an homage to that sound.

Imagine this pastiche declaimed in a deep-pitched monotone, as Ellis jiggles nonexistent jowls. He goes on to observe that during his childhood in Washington DC, "the voice that was on television all the time was Richard Nixon, and so when I began my formal training in poetry, you know, they all sounded like Nixon to me."

Thomas Sayers Ellis reads Thomas Stearns Eliot (and Williams, and Frost) as Nixon, guilty spokesman for a corrupt establishment. This is part of what modernism means now, has meant for decades: not revolutionary art but stiff authority. Despite the stiffness and the guilt, though, Ellis describes enchantment by rhythm. Ellis was beat digging, riffling through old vinyl, haunted less by the denotation of the words than by their detonations. Auden is right that moments of Eliotic influence are hard to finger, but it's precisely in cadence that Eliot's work survives.

For twenty-first-century poets, Eliot persists as a sonic obsession more vividly than as a poet who leveled important arguments or shaped literary history. As editor, critic, and builder of poetic landmarks from recycled materials, the man overshadowed Anglo-American poetry for generations. For William Carlos Williams, the atomic blast of *The Waste Land* knocked American poetry out of its groove. For poets born in the thirties and forties — Craig Raine, Wendy Cope, Derek Walcott, Seamus Heaney — Eliot is monumental, although those writers have different responses to his looming edifice. Poets born since, though, metabolized Eliot differently. It's not that modernism is less relevant. Younger writers claim certain modernist poets over and over: Williams, W.B. Yeats, Robert Frost, Gertrude Stein, Wallace Stevens, Langston Hughes, H.D., Robert Hayden, Gwendolyn Brooks. Eliot just isn't on their public lists quite so often.

The "paradigm shift" lowering Eliot's status, as David Chinitz puts it, occurred in the eighties. In 1989, Cynthia Ozick commented in *The New Yorker* on Eliot's reduced place in school curricula. Books by Christopher Ricks and, slightly later, Anthony Julius brought Eliot's anti-Semitism to the fore. Also in the late eighties, a prize-winning essay by Wayne Koestenbaum highlighted Eliot's misogynistic and homoerotic correspondence with Ezra Pound, midwife to *The Waste Land*. Eliot's poetry of the teens and twenties communicates fear of women, and often revulsion about their bodies, and Koestenbaum adds force to the point. Then there was Eliot's portrayal in the 1994 film *Tom & Viv* by Willem Dafoe, a.k.a. the Green Goblin. Eliot is a synonym for tradition but he also became, for readers attuned to his prejudices, a supervillain.

The gradual mutation of modernist reputations over time is no catastrophe. Certain poetic frequencies, strong at the time, had become buried in interference. Poet-performers such as Hughes, Amy Lowell, Edna St. Vincent Millay, Vachel Lindsay, and Carl Sandburg experimented with new performance modes and ultimately changed what we expect from poetry readings, in addition to publishing verse that hums with theatrical and musical energy — their signals should still reach us. Nor does the swelling of the modernist horde mean Eliot's resonance has died. People want to voice his poetry and hear it voiced. *Four Quartets*, for instance, is popular again, inspiring performances by Chicago actor Mike Rogalski and by Ariel Artists, a group of classical musicians that stages collaborative events.

For poets making their names now, Eliot endures as a rhythm, an icon of recurrence. His early verse offers a resource for those obsessed with linguistic music but skeptical of meter, and particularly for poets who chime radically different registers and references, hoping to revive something human through uncanny convergences. For some writers, these powerful cadences are abstracted from meaning; *The Waste Land* is an emblem of obscurity, communicating mainly the impossibility of communication. Others, though, understand the noisiness of Eliot's jazz-influenced verse as a mark and even a means of transformation. Sound is how Eliot expresses personal despair and social critique most forcefully, and also how he survives the apocalypse.

•

"Poetic sound" is a physical phenomenon and a metaphor. Voiced texts, whether performed by the author or by someone else, involve pitch, volume, duration, and all the linguistic prosody of dialect, including rhythm, stress, and intonation. Medium matters: live presence and video convey gesture, facial expression, and other visual information, while recording and broadcasting technologies introduce nonhuman noise and strip away most of what the body says. Silent reading is also a physical phenomenon, engaging muscles and parts of the brain associated with vocalization and audition. Printed, digital, or manuscript texts have other sonic attributes, too. Although recitation makes sound structures more audible, a good reader, without voicing a poem, may perceive alliteration, rhyme, and meter or other rhythmic patterns interacting with vocabulary and typography. I often seem to hear a poem as I read it silently, especially if I know the author's own voice, and most especially if that voice is unusual — Brooks's musical intonations, for example, haunt my inner ear more powerfully than Adrienne Rich's plain intensity, although both authors are deeply important to me.

Because listening to an author's recitation can change how you read a poem forever, never play Eliot's 1948 recording of "The Love Song of J. Alfred Prufrock." "Prufrock" on the page is full of discord, humor, fear, and despair, but the poet's Talking Dead performance leaches out its urgency. Listeners to the Caedmon version of *The Waste Land*, recorded in 1947 and 1955 in London, and for a long time the only widely available performance by Eliot, have often felt the same horror. This version is, however, unforgettable. My own copy is a bootleg cassette handed to me in the early nineties by my dissertation adviser, A. Walton Litz. He remarked that Eliot's recitation lasts just under half an hour, meaning, by Edgar Allen Poe's rule of duration, *The Waste Land* counts as a lyric poem. Did Walt give this peculiar gift to generations of graduate students, or did he, like Tiresias, foresee my doom?

This aural document is peculiar in several ways. Part of the strangeness rests in pronunciation. Eliot was raised in St. Louis and educated in New England when American classrooms emphasized the art of elocution. *The Waste Land* was published in 1922, but by the forties, Eliot had lived in England for decades and delivered more than fifty radio talks via the BBC. The result of all this schooling, dislocation, and re-schooling is a placeless, transatlantic sort of accent. Eliot's diction in the recording is precise, without elision unless he's performing a Cockney conversation, as in the pub argument of part two. "Indifference," for example, is a four-syllable word; "jewels" contains two. "Year" requires almost two syllables, fading out on a non-rhotic British- or New England-inflected *r*. An *r* at the beginning of a word such as "rain" sometimes receives a slight trill. He pronounces "shone" with a short *o*, "clerk" with a short *a*. Eliot's nasal voice sounds a little affected, prissy, all head.

Another peculiarity is the *unity* the poem acquires in Eliot's delivery. Originally titled "He Do the Police in Different Voices," *The Waste Land* famously contains many instances of unmarked allusion and dialogue; perspectives shift radically, without warning; languages clash. Eliot's recording does mark some of those differences. He utters certain lines with oratorical gravity but speeds up, mimics conversational rhythms in others. One striking instance of rhythmic transformation occurs within a single character's voice. Madame Sosostris mouthing prophecy, for example, sounds slower and more serious than the brisk businesswoman who brings the fortune-telling session to a close. Later, Eliot pronounces each "O O O O" before "that Shakespeherian Rag" with escalating volume and pitch, enacting distress. For the most part, though, Eliot's recording mutes disjunction.

Listening to a metrical poet read his or her work aloud can be a revelation, especially when rhetorical emphasis contradicts the apparent meter. While *The Waste Land* has many iambic passages — some of which Pound marked "too penty" in typescript — Eliot's renderings of them aren't surprising. He emphasizes rather than obscures cadences latent in print. This is also true of syntactic rhythms, such as the line-ending participles that punctuate the poem's opening: breeding, mixing, stirring. Some of the most jarring sections consist of transliterated bird song — "Jug jug jug jug jug jug" — but Eliot pronounces those, too, precisely and unmusically.

Idiosyncratic music finally enters the recitation in the "Weialala leia" lines from "The Fire Sermon," imitating, as Eliot's note tells us, the song of the Rhinemaidens in Wagner's *Götterdämmerung*. We have time traveled on the Thames, back to Elizabeth and Leicester drifting on a barge. Eliot half-sings the syllables. These vocalizations are wordless — their meanings are their music — and yet it's weird to hear this previously depressed character caroling them. So far Eliot's reading has emphasized sentence over line, correctness over play or surprise. This changes as the poem finishes. In the syntactically broken, unpunctuated opening of part five, "What the Thunder Said," Eliot allows each line break to hang in the air like a frustrated incantation. Later he sings a fragment of "London Bridge." He slows down and softens his voice for the poem's prayer-like conclusion. By now, the illusion of a single protagonist is strong, and the increasing intensity of the performance contributes to the effect. The development of the recording's acoustic texture parallels and affirms the transformation this protagonist experiences, sitting at the edge of his despair, listening to thunder herald healing.

Eliot's performance has interesting nuances, but it isn't a particularly dramatic reading, especially given the dramatic nature of the text itself and his success as a playwright. A 1935 recording available online at The Poetry Archive is deemed better — his recitations became less dynamic as years passed — but the style and cadence are fundamentally similar. Eliot's drone implies dislike of elocutionary theatrics, a common modernist sentiment, in favor of minimalist transmission. Yet Eliot could and did read in a markedly different way, most notably in his Harvard recording of "Fragment of an Agon" from an unfinished first verse drama, *Sweeney Agonistes*. Even on the page the lines seem highly rhythmic, in imitation of the music-hall jazz, vaudeville, and minstrelsy Eliot consumed avidly, but the cadence of his rapid, comic delivery is even more extraordinary. His delivery is accentual rather than metrical, imitating the flexible three- and four-beat lines of popular song with variable numbers of syllables between heavy stresses ("A NICE little, WHITE little, MISSionary STEW"). He even syncopates, stressing occasional off-beats ("Wear PALMleaf DRAPerY"). Genre distinctions partially explain Eliot's striking change in recitation style. *Sweeney Agonistes* is drama and therefore uses what Eliot calls poetry's "third voice," character-based speech. In the essay "The Three Voices of Poetry," Eliot distinguishes verse drama from what he calls the first voice of "meditative verse," meaning "the voice of the poet talking to himself—or to nobody," and from the second voice of persona poetry, in which one hears both poet and mask. The conceptually different voice of "Fragment" translates into a different authorial voicing. Still, the existence of the latter demonstrates that Eliot's far flatter performance of *The Waste Land* was a *choice*.

One final detail about *The Waste Land* as its author sounded it: Eliot strips away the anti-poetic apparatus scaffolding the poem. A performance of the notes would be bizarre, but Eliot does not even read the epigraph or dedication—he frees *The Waste Land* from its scholarly frame. Hearing all the poem's perspectives channeled through Eliot's own peculiar accent illuminates this work as a lyric meditation, an expressive "piece of rhythmical grumbling," as Eliot later claimed and Walt Litz advised me. Its motive and meaning root deeply, as lyric does by definition, in sound.

•

The resonance of *The Waste Land*, now as in Auden's time, can be as faint and intermittent as a radio signal in the mountains. Major Jackson would seem likely to channel Eliotic echoes; he's an allusive, sound-oriented writer who, like Eliot, mixes references from a wide range of registers. In an interview with Chris Tonelli for *Redivider*, Jackson remarks:

> The re-mix honors the original; so much of our daily lives is inauthentic. The collage, the sample, the remix, gumbo, all work to recontextualize and reinvigorate how we experience and taste the world around us.... The remix allows us to view standards (and yes, even our clichéd lives) with new sets of eyewear or earwear. T.S. Eliot sampled. Bearden re-mixed. It's the great, modernist trick. The thing to remember also is that this is how the past manifests itself in the present, how it influences and yields New Art, how it extends the conversation.

I wrote to Jackson in 2012 to ask what Eliot means to him, and his comments echo those earlier ones:

Indeed, Eliot was an early influence. Both *The Waste Land* and "Preludes" (and to a lesser degree such canonized poems as "Prufrock," "Ash Wednesday," etc.) lit a way for me to be highly allusive, especially with pop culture, but more importantly, his rhythmic changes and meters authorized a similar approach to composing poems.

In the fall of 2011, too, Jackson participated in a performance of *Four Quartets* with Ariel Artists and the Iktus Percussion quartet in Vermont, reciting passages of "Burnt Norton" in concert with other voices and instruments.

Jackson's poetic references to Eliot, however, are slight and fleeting. My favorite of Jackson's works, "Letter to Brooks," a sixty-page epistle to the Chicago poet in rime royal, name-checks an astonishing number of twentieth-century poets. Eliot is not among them, although Jackson declares an urban "wasteland" can be a crucial inspiration for a poet. Jackson's most recent book, *Holding Company*, begins with an epigraph not from the modernist poet but about him, via Robert Lowell's unrhymed sonnet "T.S. Eliot." Lowell's elegy represents the circulation of names, talk, and influence within American poetry. Eliot may be "lost in the dark night of the brilliant talkers," but this is a starry afterlife full of friendly constellations. By quoting Lowell on Eliot, Jackson enters that exchange. But after the epigraph, where is Old Possum? *Holding Company* begins, "For I was born, too, in the stunted winter of History," and references "valleys of corpses," gardens, soft broken ground, sensations of desire and loss. These images resonate with "The Burial of the Dead," but given that Jackson also uses the phrase "I, too" twice, Langston Hughes and Walt Whitman seem more obvious sources of inspiration. Imagery follows of war, painful Aprils, city streets, Greek myth, infernos, ruins, lovers unable to communicate, thirst and water — the vocabulary of *The Waste Land* is certainly in Jackson's blender. Sometimes he gets closer to direct allusion, as in "Recondite": "He connects with nothing. One imagines him/picking scars in the river." We're almost floating on the Thames with Elizabeth and Leicester or connecting nothing with nothing on Margate Sands, but the echo is weak, and the poem, to use Jackson's word, recondite. There's a sense that *The Waste Land* matters, but the *matter* of it doesn't.

•

In *Lucifer at the Starlite*, Eliot definitely plays on Kim Addonizio's juke-box, and not as background music. Addonizio's subjects are similar to Eliot's before his conversion. She portrays an infernal world full of debased sex, pointless violence, exhilarating art, and profound isola-tion. For her, though, *The Waste Land* is a sort of zombie poem, sham-bling dangerously into your ear and emanating the stink of perdition.

"Now recite/*The Waste Land*, backwards,/beginning with that sexy Sanskrit word": her poem "Yes," a mock-questionnaire for po-tential alcoholics, ends with the sobriety test from hell. Addonizio references the famous difficulty of Eliot's poem ("Now recite 'The Road Not Taken'" would kill the joke). *The Waste Land* offers a test of the reader's erudition and interpretive powers, a competitive ex-ercise rather than an emotional or intellectual experience. Fail and lose your poetic license. That it stands in for the usual demand to recite the alphabet in reverse suggests how fundamental *The Waste Land* is but reinforces its obscurity, too. *The Waste Land* constitutes a basic linguistic resource but is not intelligible in itself, backwards or forwards. Addonizio's poem concerns addiction and depression, though, and while she doesn't draw the connection explicitly, she implicitly identifies *The Waste Land* with those experiences. "That empty feeling crawling toward you" is an Eliotic monster, more in-sectile than the rodents dragging their slimy bellies along the banks of the Thames, but still embodying despair in a personal serving size.

Addonizio's "The First Line Is the Deepest" links "The Love Song of J. Alfred Prufrock" to the longer poem's apocalyptic mood. Instead of measuring out sweetness in her life with Prufrock's coffee spoons, Addonizio's speaker doses herself into polite behavior with "little pills — Zoloft,//Restoril, Celexa,/Xanax." What's at stake is essentially personal suffering, although brand names indicate how psychic pain, sleeplessness, and anxiety are currently defined as con-sumer issues with well-advertised remedies. "The First Line Is the Deepest" later reframes the famous first line of *The Waste Land* as a question: "Why does one month have to be the cruelest,/can't they all be equally cruel?" Coming right after a reference to Halliburton and right before an allusion to single-player shooter games, this tune is actually the dullest she spins. *The Waste Land* inspires anxiety and irritable questioning. Again, it's that empty feeling crawling toward you. She swats it to death in the final sentences with Allen Ginsberg's passion and Robert Frost's beautiful misanthropy.

·

Robert Sullivan is a very different poet than Addonizio: talkier, more overtly and consistently political, witty in a quieter register. He shares, however, her attitude of listening; a strange assortment of voices loops through their brains, and both poets represent that mix with high fidelity. His 2005 collection *Voice Carried My Family* shifts between Maori and English, considering history, religion, and literature in quick succession. Sullivan worries over how colonialism has changed his relationship to language. While he identifies his family and heritage with physical voice, here he is working ambitiously in the medium of print. Writing the pronoun "I," possessing a print self, may in itself constitute a betrayal of his family — and his desire to transcribe family stories and retell Pacific history worsens the problem. Several poems in *Voice Carried My Family* embody this conflict in his "shadow." This word has a religious dimension, meaning something like spirit, but it also gestures toward the literary doppelgänger he resembles, wants to like, but must distrust.

Sullivan's "13 ways of looking at a blackbirder" invokes a range of precursor texts, including the famous Wallace Stevens poem and *Peter Pan*. It also refers to, without glossing, a different meaning for "blackbird" than Stevens had in mind. Blackbirding, a widespread practice in the Pacific in the late nineteenth century, means tricking or kidnapping indigenous people to provide plantation labor. Sullivan imagines, "I must have signed a contract in my sleep/with a blackbirding devil/that nailed this shadow to my hands and feet." This shadow or literary self is a manifestation of his enslavement.

A few sections later, though, he strips off that nailed-on double, retaining only a more natural shadow, portrayed here as a valuable gift handed down from his parents:

> XII
> in the purging wasteland shantihs
> let peace rain down and sink the blackbirders
> claw off the nailed shadow from me

> XIII
> free at last from irony and its grating
> I have my shadow back
> the one stitched to me by my mother and father
> the one handed down *tuku iho tuku iho*

Somehow, a monumental and distinctly literary work becomes the instrument of peace. The reference flits by quickly, but Sullivan reads *The Waste Land* as a sincere poem of suffering and release. Interestingly, Sullivan inhabits not the waste land but the *shantihs* — that sexy Sanskrit word. Salvation and freedom lie in a return to family but also in the restorative sound of repeated syllables.

·

In *The Waste Land and Other Poems*, John Beer takes allusion to its limit, revisiting the modernist monument as if possessed by Eliot's ghost. The book's first poem, "Sound of Water Over a Rock," empties Eliot's poetry of meaning in favor of its tantalizing sounds. Beer refers to the hermit-thrush song in "What the Thunder Said," the final section of *The Waste Land*. Its trill mocks refreshment in Eliot's dead landscape: "Drip drop drip drop drop drop drop/But there is no water." Beer's response to Eliot's prompt is three pages of quatrains, 448 words in all, consisting entirely of the syllables "drip" and "drop." In Eliot's original poem, sound is separated from reality by a frustratingly arid gulf. By stripping context from the birdsong's transliteration, Beer amplifies and extends its implicit taunt. This is a dead world, without consolation.

Stephen Burt calls Beer's book "anti-lyrical." Beer's idiosyncratic homage-parody-mirror-critique certainly challenges any association of poetry with self-expression. Eliot sampled and remixed sources, but for him the original works of art retained great power. In Beer, allusion resembles the visual experience of *mise en abyme*: if poetry ever could conjure something fresh and real, it's an embedded speck now, carried out to sea by a tide of echoes. Yet somehow the illusion of voice is strong in Beer's "The Waste Land." His poem's long first sentence invites us into the author's associative dream. Scenes such as being sneered at in the Princeton Record Exchange are familiar, funny, and grounding. He conveys an intensely personal desperation at the unreality of the present world, the inadequacy of words. Eliot's rhymes and phrasings become shorthand for the debasement of language and experience, but they also conduct a vivid sense of urgency.

·

"No song can bear/the weight we need to place upon it;/nothing returns as we ask it to return," Beer writes from the "discount bin." I teach Eliot's *The Waste Land* yearly and every time I pick it up, it sounds more extravagantly gothic. Its images and rhythms captured my ear when I was an undergraduate in the late eighties, full of fashionable contempt for received forms and unable to admit how much poetic sound mattered to me. I was hooked by Eliot's irreverent chiming not only of syllables and languages but of cultural extremes — Shakespeare and ragtime, personal crisis and public trauma, Greek myth and Bram Stoker. When *The Waste Land* returned to me in middle age, began whispering new lines in my mind's ear, it was reborn as a zombie apocalypse tale. I was headed to Pittsburgh for Thanksgiving at a particularly disastrous moment for my husband's clan: relatives were eating each other's brains and I saw omens of worsening infestation. My in-laws live very near the Monroeville Mall, where George A. Romero filmed *Dawn of the Dead*. *The Walking Dead* was on TV and I had just received *Pride and Prejudice and Zombies* for my birthday. I saw revenants everywhere.

In *The Waste Land*, Eliot, like any vampire slayer, desires and fears to reanimate the dead. Tarot cards, ghosts, sprouting corpses, mythic transformations, potions in vials, chuckling skeletons, baby-faced bats, voices singing from exhausted wells — *The Waste Land* is, among many other things, a horror story. Zombie horror involves bodies without minds or souls, terror that we might only be bodies caught up in meaningless rhythms of predation and digestion, that the goodness we aspire to is all just empty ritual. Composing my own poetic riff on *The Waste Land* made me consider what all plague survivors wonder about the undead. Beyond the familiar rotting visage, is anything human left?

•

For the youngest poet in this playlist, the answer is: stop worrying about stupid questions and *listen*. In slam pieces such as "William Shakespeare Gets Hooked on 8-Bit Nintendo" and "Sylvia Plath's Gangsta Rap Legacy," Jeremy Richards responds to pop culture through the diction, tropes, and rhythms of super-canonical poets. Richards's Plath, for example, declares, "Mack Daddy you do not do." The satire is so silly and deadpan, and so stylistically thorough, it becomes serious again. For these parody-homages, Richards chooses writers whose textual performances of self are especially layered. While Plath's poems seem to collapse the distance between poet and speaker, for instance, her frequent gestures to a "peanut-crunching crowd" keep reframing the apparently expressive personal lyric as a circus. Hers makes a good position from which to mock the stagey misogyny of gangsta rap — and the similarly ritualistic critique of that misogyny.

The seriousness culturally attached to Plath is quite different than Eliot's high-culture, pinstripe-suit seriousness, but it can have the same result: deadening what's theatrical and funny about the writing, muting its catchy wit. Richards turns up the volume again, putting Eliot's verse in conversation with popular song in "T.S. Eliot's Lost Hip Hop Poem," correlating Eliot's extremely white persona with the sound and sense of an African-American form. In fact, these connections are already latent in Eliot's verse, though Pound edited most of the jazz out of early versions of *The Waste Land*. Eliot wrote in *The Use of Poetry and the Use of Criticism* that the "auditory imagination" involves "returning to the origin and bringing something back" — even the prose becomes iambic when he considers poetry's roots in music. Eliot's writing, at its best, reflects his own omnivorous listening in St. Louis, Boston, and London.

I'm not claiming "T.S. Eliot's Lost Hip Hop Poem" as a twenty-first-century literary monument to parallel *The Waste Land*, but Richards's poem taps similar sources. In a recorded performance, Richards hunches over to assume the Ancient Modernist Persona and samples Eliot with nerdy fervor. He begins with a strong echo of "Prufrock" — "Let us roll then, you and I" — but quickly folds in a range of other conventions and references. An allusion to Lazarus yields to the command "Bring the bass," beatboxing by Nathan Ramos, and the demand "Who's your daddy now?" in Russian. Mimicking Eliot's precise articulation, Richards rhymes "reign" with "again" and trills the *r* in "Bring the pathos!" Behind the camera, the audience laughs and shouts approval as he collapses the gap between modernism and spoken word.

Richards's remix is an exuberant assertion of personal erudition resembling those by Addonizio, Beer, and Eliot himself, but inflected with rap braggadocio ("the evening stretched out against the sky/like a punk ass I laid out with my phat rhymes"). It is a canon-making gesture like Eliot's own — a declaration that we must not allow these poems to slide into obscurity as vitality leaves the page for the stage.

Richards also levels the implicit argument that self is performance, and a good performance survives through cadence, a sonic hook snagged in neural tissue.

Like all the other poets discussed here, Richards obsesses over loneliness and mortality. These were not fresh subjects in Eliot's time, and they're not dead ones in ours, although they can get a little stiff when writers and readers treat poetry too reverentially. To echo Major Jackson, an audacious remix revives the past and enables us to "taste" the present differently. Eliot's work may be rotten in spots but persists vigorously; his own remix remains infectious. Rhythm is recurrence, the repetition of some element over time. While we breathe, the beat can still entrain us.

CONTRIBUTORS

JOHN ASHBERY's new book of poems, *Breezeway* (Ecco), will be published next year. A two-volume set of his translations (poetry and prose) was published in early 2014 by Farrar, Straus and Giroux.

SUSAN BARBA* is a poet, translator, and editor at *New York Review Books*. She lives in Cambridge, Massachusetts.

AMY BEEDER's books are *Now Make an Altar* (2012) and *Burn the Field* (2006), both published by Carnegie Mellon University Press. She lives in New Mexico.

HENRI COLE's new collection, *Nothing to Declare*, is forthcoming from Farrar, Straus and Giroux. He teaches at Ohio State University.

ROBERT FERNANDEZ* is the author of *Pink Reef* (2013) and *We Are Pharaoh* (2011), both published by Canarium Books. The poems in this issue are from his forthcoming book, *Crowns*.

CATHERINE FIELD lives in Carbondale, Illinois and is active in community organizations promoting peace, justice, and the arts.

FRANCINE J. HARRIS* is the author of *allegiance* (Wayne State University Press, 2012). Originally from Detroit, she is a Cave Canem Fellow and a writer-in-residence at Front Street Writers.

DOUGLAS KEARNEY's third poetry collection, *Patter* (Red Hen Press, 2014) examines miscarriage, infertility, and parenthood. *The Black Automaton* (Fence Books, 2009), was a National Poetry Series selection. He teaches at CalArts.

JOHN KOETHE's most recent book is *ROTC Kills* (Harper Perennial, 2012). A new book, *The Swimmer*, will be published by Farrar, Straus and Giroux in 2016.

SYLVIA LEGRIS's* most recent publication is *Pneumatic Antiphonal* (New Directions, 2013). Her third book, *Nerve Squall* (Coach House Books, 2005), won the 2006 Griffin Poetry Prize.

DANA LEVIN's most recent book is *Sky Burial* (Copper Canyon Press, 2011). Levin teaches at Santa Fe University of Art and Design.

D. NURKSE's most recent book is *A Night in Brooklyn* (Knopf, 2012).

ROWAN RICARDO PHILLIPS* is the author of *The Ground* (Farrar, Straus and Giroux, 2012). His second book of poems, *Heaven*, will be published by Farrar, Straus and Giroux in 2015.

KAY RYAN's most recent book is *The Best of It: New and Selected Poems* (Grove Press, 2010).

STEPHEN SANDY's recent books are *Overlook* (Louisiana State University Press, 2010), *Netsuke Days* (Shires Press, 2008), and *Weathers Permitting* (Louisiana State University Press, 2005).

SONNENZIMMER* is the Chicago-based studio of Nick Butcher and Nadine Nakanishi. Their practice merges fine art, printmaking, graphic design, sound art, and publishing.

ARTHUR VOGELSANG's *Expedition: New and Selected Poems* appeared from Ashland Poetry Press in 2011.

ALLI WARREN* is the author of *Here Come the Warm Jets* (City Lights, 2013) as well as several chapbooks. She edits the magazine *Dreamboat* and coedits the Poetic Labor Project blog.

NOAH WARREN* was born in Antigonish, Nova Scotia, and is living in New Orleans. His work has appeared in *The Yale Review* and elsewhere.

LESLEY WHEELER's poetry collections are *The Receptionist and Other Tales* (Aqueduct Press, 2012), *Heterotopia* (Barrow Street Press, 2010), and *Heathen* (C&R Press, 2009). She teaches at Washington and Lee University in Virginia.

* First appearance in *Poetry.*

Peter Porter Poetry Prize 2015

The 2015 Peter Porter Poetry Prize is now open. The Prize is for a new poem of up to 75 lines and is open to all poets writing in English around the world.

Prize money
The Prize is worth AU$7,500.
The winner will receive AU$5,000.
All six shortlisted poems will be published
in *Australian Book Review*.

Judges
Lisa Gorton (*ABR* Poetry Editor), Paul Kane (Vassar College), and Peter Rose (*ABR* Editor)

Entries close
15 December 2014

Full details and online entry can be found on our website: www.australianbookreview.com.au

ABR publishes new poems throughout the year, from poets such as John Ashbery, Les Murray, Jennifer Maiden, Clive James, Fleur Adcock, Simon Armitage, Stephen Edgar and John Kinsella.

We welcome electronic submissions via email:
poetry@australianbookreview.com.au

Be sure to visit *ABR Online*!

Free 3-day trial access to the latest issue
$40 for 1 year
$25 for those 25 and under
$6 for 30 days

www.australianbookreview.com.au

Read *Poetry*

SOUTHWEST ✦ REVIEW

2014 Morton Marr Poetry Prize

FIRST PLACE – $1,000
SECOND PLACE – $500

PUBLICATION IN *Southwest Review*
ACCOMPANIES BOTH PRIZES

- Open to writers who have not yet published a book of poetry.
- Submission of no more than six, previously unpublished, poems in a "traditional" form (e.g., sonnet, sestina, villanelle, rhymed stanzas, blank verse, et al.).
- Poems should be printed blank with name and address information only on a cover sheet or letter.
- $5.00 per poem entry/handling fee.
- Postmarked deadline for entry is September 30, 2014.
- Submissions will not be returned. All entrants will receive a copy of the issue in which the winning poems appear.
- Mail entry to: The Morton Marr Poetry Prize, Southwest Review, P.O. Box 750374, Dallas, TX 75275-0374

Visit us at www.smu.edu/southwestreview

THE POETRY FOUNDATION'S Harriet Monroe Poetry Institute's

POETS IN THE WORLD

series edited by Ilya Kaminsky

Anglophone Poetry
Tupelo Press
Catherine Barnett and Tiphanie Yanique

World Poetry
Open Letter Books
Eliot Weinberger

Iraqi Poetry
New Directions
Dunya Mikhail

Chinese Poetry
Tupelo Press
Ming Di

Swedish Poetry
Milkweed Editions
Malena Mörling and Jonas Ellerström

Latin American Poetry
Copper Canyon Press
Raúl Zurita and Forrest Gander

**African Continent
Poetry**
Slapering Hol Press
Kwame Dawes and Chris Abani

**European Continent
Poetry**
Red Hen Press
Valzhyna Mort

**Poets Writing
Across Borders**
McSweeney's Books
*Jared Hawkley, Susan Rich
and Brian Turner*

The *Poets in the World* series offers English-speaking audiences a rare glimpse at the work of poets who have shaped literary traditions from around the globe, from Africa to Europe, Iraq to China, and beyond. *Poets in the World*, a project of the Poetry Foundation's Harriet Monroe Poetry Institute, collaborates with a wide range of American publishers to produce beautiful publications that advance readership for world poetry.

www.poetryfoundation.org/institute

POETRY
FOUNDATION

THE POETRY FOUNDATION PRESENTS

September Events

Reading	**Lambda Literary Foundation:** **Launch of *Nepantla: A Journal Dedicated to* *Queer Poets of Color*** Thursday, September 4 at 7:00 PM
Poetry & *Music*	**Collaborative Arts Institute of Chicago's** **Salon Concert: Schumann, Rückert & Heine** Thursday, September 11 at 7:00 PM
The Open Door *Reading Series*	**DePaul's Chris Green & Loyola's Aaron Baker** Highlights outstanding writing programs in the Chicago area. Tuesday, September 16 at 7:00 PM
Reading	**Guild Complex: Ana Castillo, Paul Martínez** **Pompa & Cristina Correa** Wednesday, September 17 at 7:00 PM
Celebratory *Reading*	**Graywolf Press 40th Anniversary:** **Claudia Rankine, Matthea Harvey & Katie Ford** Thursday, September 18 at 7:00 PM
Poetry & *Music*	***Freedom of Shadow: A Tribute to Terry Adkins*** **with libretto by Douglas Kearney** Saturday, September 20 at 6:00 PM
Reading & *Conversation*	**Todd Swift & John Wilkinson** Reading from their work and discussing the state of contemporary British poetry. Tuesday, September 23 at 7:00 PM
Reading & *Conversation*	**Giacomo Leopardi: Jonathan Galassi,** **Michael Caesar & Franco D'Intino** Thursday, September 25 at 7:00 PM In partnership with Istituto Italiano di Cultura. Catered by Eataly.

POETRY FOUNDATION
61 West Superior Street, Chicago, IL
(312) 787-7070

www.poetryfoundation.org